W9-BTL-339

THE SWEAT OF THEIR BROW
Occupations in the 1800s

DAILY LIFE IN AMERICA IN THE 1800s

Bleeding, Blistering, and Purging: Health and Medicine in the 1800s
Buggies, Bicycles, and Iron Horses: Transportation in the 1800s
Cornmeal and Cider: Food and Drink in the 1800s
America at War: Military Conflicts at Home and Abroad in the 1800s
From the Parlor to the Altar: Romance and Marriage in the 1800s
Guardians of the Home: Women's Lives in the 1800s
Home Sweet Home: Around the House in the 1800s
Jump Ropes, Jacks, and Endless Chores: Children's Lives in the 1800s
Reviving the Spirit, Reforming Society: Religion in the 1800s
Outlaws and Lawmen: Crime and Punishment in the 1800s
Passing the Time: Entertainment in the 1800s
Rooting for the Home Team: Sports in the 1800s
Scandals and Glory: Politics in the 1800s
The Sweat of Their Brow: Occupations in the 1800s
Saloons, Shootouts, and Spurs: The Wild West In the 1800s

THE SWEAT OF THEIR BROW
Occupations in the 1800s

by

Zachary Chastain

Mason Crest Publishers

MASON CREST PUBLISHERS INC.
370 Reed Road
Broomall, Pennsylvania 19008
(866)MCP-BOOK (toll free)
www.masoncrest.com

First Printing
9 8 7 6 5 4 3 2 1

Library of Congress Cataloging-in-Publication Data

Chastain, Zachary.
The sweat of their brow : occupations in the 1800s / by Zachary Chastain.
p. cm. — (Daily life in america in the 1800s)
Includes bibliographical references and index.
ISBN 978-1-4222-1788-7 (hardcover) ISBN (series) 978-1-4222-1774-0
ISBN 978-1-4222-1861-7 (pbk.) ISBN (pbk series) 978-1-4222-1847-1
1. Occupations—United States—History—19th century. 2. Job descriptions—United States—History—19th century. I. Title.
HF5382.5.U5C488 2011
331.700973'09034—dc22
2010016869

Produced by Harding House Publishing Service, Inc.
www.hardinghousepages.com
Interior Design by MK Bassett-Harvey.
Cover design by Torque Advertising + Design.
Printed in USA by Bang Printing.

Contents

Introduction

History can too often seem a parade of distant figures whose lives have no connection to our own. It need not be this way, for if we explore the history of the games people play, the food they eat, the ways they transport themselves, how they worship and go to war—activities common to all generations—we close the gap between past and present. Since the 1960s, historians have learned vast amounts about daily life in earlier periods. This superb series brings us the fruits of that research, thereby making meaningful the lives of those who have gone before.

The authors' vivid, fascinating descriptions invite young readers to journey into a past that is simultaneously strange and familiar. The 1800s were different, but, because they experienced the beginnings of the same baffling modernity were are still dealing with today, they are also similar. This was the moment when millennia of agrarian existence gave way to a new urban, industrial era. Many of the things we take for granted, such as speed of transportation and communication, bewildered those who were the first to behold the steam train and the telegraph. Young readers will be interested to learn that growing up then was no less confusing and difficult then than it is now, that people were no more in agreement on matters of religion, marriage, and family then than they are now.

We are still working through the problems of modernity, such as environmental degradation, that people in the nineteenth century experienced for the first time. Because they met the challenges with admirable ingenuity, we can learn much from them. They left behind a treasure trove of alternative living arrangements, cultures, entertainments, technologies, even diets that are even more relevant today. Students cannot help but be intrigued, not just by the technological ingenuity of those times, but by the courage of people who forged new frontiers, experimented with ideas and social arrangements. They will be surprised by the degree to which young people were engaged in the great events of the time, and how women joined men in the great adventures of the day.

When history is viewed, as it is here, from the bottom up, it becomes clear just how much modern America owes to the genius of ordinary people, to the labor of slaves and immigrants, to women as well as men, to both young people and adults. Focused on home and family life, books in this series provide insight into how much of history is made within the intimate spaces of private life rather than in the remote precincts of public power. The 1800s were the era of the self-made man and women, but also of the self-made communities. The past offers us a plethora of heroes and heroines together with examples of extraordinary collective action from the Underground Railway to the creation of the American trade union movement. There is scarcely an immigrant or ethic organization in America today that does not trace its origins to the nineteenth century.

This series is exceptionally well illustrated. Students will be fascinated by the images of both rural and urban life; and they will be able to find people their own age in these marvelous depictions of play as well as work. History is best when it engages our imagination, draws us out of our own time into another era, allowing us to return to the present with new perspectives on ourselves. My first engagement with the history of daily life came in sixth grade when my teacher, Mrs. Polster, had us do special projects on the history of the nearby Erie Canal. For the first time, history became real to me. It has remained my passion and my compass ever since.

The value of this series is that it opens up a dialogue with a past that is by no means dead and gone but lives on in every dimension of our daily lives. When history texts focus exclusively on political events, they invariably produce a sense of distance. This series creates the opposite effect by encouraging students to see themselves in the flow of history. In revealing the degree to which people in the past made their own history, students are encouraged to imagine themselves as being history-makers in their own right. The realization that history is not something apart from ourselves, a parade that passes us by, but rather an ongoing pageant in which we are all participants, is both exhilarating and liberating, one that connects our present not just with the past but also to a future we are responsible for shaping.

—Dr. John Gillis, Rutgers University Professor of History Emeritus

Time Line

1800

1800 The Library of Congress is established.

1801

1801 Thomas Jefferson is elected as the third President of the United States.

1803

1803 Louisiana Purchase—The United States purchases land from France and begins westward exploration.

1804

1804 Journey of Lewis and Clark—Lewis and Clark lead a team of explorers westward to the Columbia River in Oregon.

1825

1825 The Erie Canal is completed—This allows direct transportation between the Great Lakes and the Atlantic Ocean.

1826

1826 Construction begins on the Pennsylvania Canal, which will link cities across the state.

1827

1827 Freedom's Journal, the first African-American owned and operated newspaper, begins publication.

1838

1838 Trail of Tears—General Winfield Scott and 7,000 troops force Cherokees to walk from Georgia to a reservation set up for them in Oklahoma (nearly 1,000 miles). Around 4,000 Native Americans die during the journey.

1812

1812 War of 1812—Fought between the United States and the United Kingdom.

1820

1820 Missouri Compromise—Agreement passes between pro-slavery and abolitionist groups, stating that all the Louisiana Purchase territory north of the southern boundary of Missouri (except for Missouri) will be free states, and the territory south of that line will be slave.

1823

1823 Monroe Doctrine—States that any efforts made by Europe to colonize or interfere with land owned by the United States will be viewed as aggression and require military intervention.

1823 The first textile mill to employ mostly women opens in what will become a network of mills in Lowell, MA.

of the 1800s

1840

1840 Baltimore College of Dental Surgery, the first dental school in the world, is founded. It becomes a model for future dental schools.

1842

1842 The Massachusetts Supreme Court decides that labor unions are not, by nature, illegal conspiracies in Commonwealth v. Hunt case.

1844

1844 First public telegraph line in the world is opened—between Baltimore and Washington.

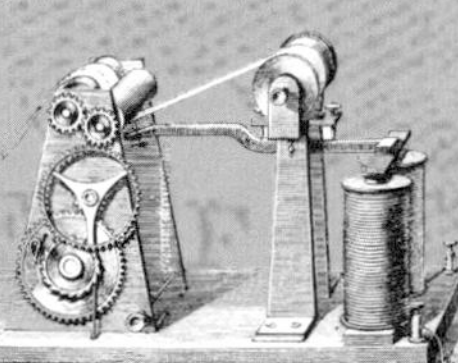

1848

1848 Seneca Falls Convention—Feminist convention held for women's suffrage and equal legal rights.

1848(-58) California Gold Rush—Over 300,000 people flock to California in search of gold.

1848 Pennsylvania passes law that sets minimum working age for children at 12.

Time Line

1854

1854 Kansas-Nebraska Act—States that each new state entering the country will decide for themselves whether or not to allow slavery. This goes directly against the terms agreed upon in the Missouri Compromise of 1820.

1861

1861(-65) Civil War —Fought between the Union and Confederate states.

1862

1862 Emancipation Proclamation—Lincoln states that all slaves in Union states are to be freed.

1865

1865 Thirteenth Amendment to the United States Constitution—Officially abolishes slavery across the country.

1865 President Abraham Lincoln is assassinated on April 15.

1876

1876 Alexander Graham Bell invents the telephone.

1877

1877 Bell Telephone Company is founded.

1877 Great Railroad Strike—Often considered the country's first nationwide labor strike.

1878

1878 Thomas Edison patents the phonograph on February 19.

1878 Thomas Edison invents the light bulb on October 22.

1884

1884 The U.S. Congress establishes the Bureau of Labor on June 27. It is tasked with gathering information about employment and labor.

1867

1867 United States purchases Alaska from Russia.

1868

1868 The U.S. government mandates maximum eight-hour day for all Federal workers.

1869

1869 Trans-continental Railroad completed on May 10.

1870

1870 Fifteenth Amendment to the United States Constitution—Prohibits any citizen from being denied to vote based on their "race, color, or previous condition of servitude."

1870 Christmas is declared a national holiday.

of the 1800s

1886

1886 The Statue of Liberty is dedicated on October 28.

1886 The American Federation of Labor (AFL) is formed in Columbus, Ohio.

1890

1890 Wounded Knee Massacre—Last battle in the American Indian Wars.

1892

1892 Ellis Island is opened to receive immigrants coming into New York.

1896

1896 Plessy vs. Ferguson—Supreme Court case that rules that racial segregation is legal as long as accommodations are kept equal.

1896 Henry Ford builds his first combustion-powered vehicle, which he names the Ford Quadricycle.

1898

1898 The Spanish-American War—The United States gains control of Cuba, Puerto Rico, and the Philippines.

Part I
From Farm to City

Thomas Jefferson, president from 1801 to 1809, once wrote in a letter to James Madison, "The small land holders are the most precious part of a state." When Jefferson was president, he did everything in his power to uphold what he saw as the backbone of the new American nation: small farmers.

This was a policy that worked quite well because, at the time of Jefferson's presidency, the majority of Americans were small farmers. Even the pioneers settling the Western frontier did so in the hopes of owning a piece of land. Of course, farms varied in size—from the large tobacco plantations of the South to the small plots owned by freed slaves and poor whites in both the North and the South.

Farm jobs typically involved every member of a family. There were animals to care for; crops to plant, protect, and harvest; and farm products to make, like cheese and bread. Many women were skilled in domestic arts such as sewing and basket weaving, medicine making, and fine needlework of all kinds. These were products used primarily at home, but were occasionally brought to market or used to trade for other goods the family might need. Most people participated in farm economies where they traded and borrowed for what they needed to survive.

Educated Men

Some men did have an opportunity to choose their own occupation, but these were few, and the professions to choose from even fewer (nothing like the choices available at today's colleges, where students can choose from hundreds of courses of study). In the early 1800s, only a few universities had been established, and those lucky enough to attend them almost always came from wealthy backgrounds. Generally, a young man from a middle- or upper-class family would study law, medicine,

Middle-class men in the nineteenth century sometimes worked in offices, running various kinds of business.

Clergymen were usually educated in seminaries, but some of them were self-taught.

or go to seminary to become a clergyman. Those middle- and upper-class men who didn't go to university usually inherited the family business from their fathers. These were merchants who owned fleets of ships, distributed goods, and controlled commerce between states and nations.

In the East, young children and girls were taught by women, but men generally taught classes of boys. (On the frontier, however, women taught both boys and girls.)

Doctors

In the early 1800s, most doctors weren't trained at universities. For the most part, doctors were still trained the way they'd been trained for hundreds of years: by other doctors. Young men learned by following or "shadowing" another doctor on visits to patients' homes. The older doctor was the younger man's teacher, giving him opportunities to practice his skills under the older doctor's watchful eye. Because there was no license that doctors had to apply for, anyone with experience could try his hand at medicine.

In those days, doctors came to visit the patients, rarely the other way around. They didn't have the science to fully understand germs, or a variety of other ideas that doctors today use to heal people. Visits were often for a fever or a cold, which were common killers in those days. A doctor's job was largely to give medicines and advice, and occasionally perform a surgery if necessary. Often, the medicines didn't work, and the surgeries were based on understandings of the body that have since been proven false.

In the 1800s, doctors made house calls. Upper-class young women sometimes suffered from "vapors," a condition that was characterized mostly by weakness. Historians speculate that many of these women may have been suffering from conditions that would today be labeled depression, PMS, or other psychiatric disorders such as bipolar disorder. Some historians speculate that women's fashions may have been responsible as well—wearing tight corsets cut off women's circulation and prevented them from getting enough oxygen.

The success of the treatment depended on the doctor. Some doctors practiced "herbal" or "irregular" medicine, which was thought of as strange at the time because it used plants and herbs to heal instead of the "regular" theories of the day. Most physicians used a combination of herbal medicine and the "Four Humors" system of the human body. This system believed there were four types of elements or "humors" in the body, and that sick people had an improper balance of those elements. So sometimes physicians gave patients a small cut and let them bleed a while, believing this would restore balance to their bodies. In fact, blood loss weakened already sick people and often killed them.

This device (above) was used by nineteenth-century doctors for bloodletting.

This drawing (below) shows some of the "tools" doctors used for bloodletting: knives, cups, and leeches, a kind of worm that when placed on a person's skin would suck his blood.

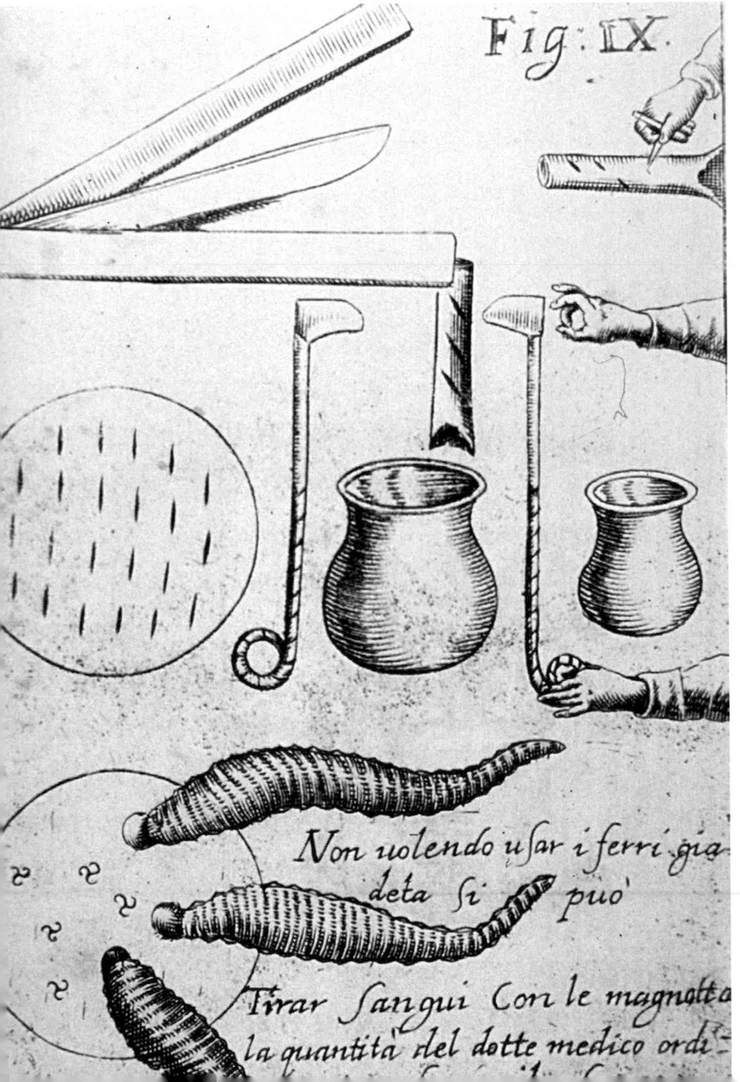

Women at Work

In the early 1800s, women were, for the most part, expected to remain at home. The household was the woman's domain, and in it she reigned supreme. At almost every level of society, women were excluded from jobs and tasks of every kind. This didn't mean that women were without influence, however. Since the country's birth, American women had worked alongside their male counterparts. America was, after all, built on the backs of immigrants in a foreign land. People arriving in a new land and trying to survive couldn't afford to exclude women—their skills and labor were simply too valuable!

But as time wore on, and the 1800s saw the "civilization" of the American frontier, more and more settlers sough to establish the "Old World" gender system. In fact, European traditions of all kinds persisted throughout the 1800s. Many wealthy Americans (and those aspiring to wealth) tried to imitate and preserve the lifestyles of England and Europe. It was a mark of pride among classes both rich and poor that a successful family was one in which the woman was able to remain at home.

Many nineteenth-century women helped with the labor on the farms where they lived.

In the 1800s, women from families who wanted to be considered "upper class" often lived lives of leisure, where fashion and socializing occupied much of their time.

As the upper class was established during the 1800s in America, some women worked as servants in the homes of rich families.

Women and Education

Those families who could afford it might send their daughters to one of the handful of women's colleges for what was basically a "ladylike" education. Emphasizing singing, literature, religion, and dancing, these schools prepared a woman more for marriage and motherhood than for a profession. Some women did train at seminary to become teachers, but this was generally considered an unmarried profession, unsuitable for wives and mothers.

Unmarried women worked as teachers, but they were usually expected to quit once they married.

Though they weren't called doctors, many women were already acting as doctors and nurses by the early 1800s. The practice of medicine by women was usually known by another name—midwifery. American midwifery became well established during the Revolutionary War, when doctors trained women to assist them in healing wounded soldiers, but midwifery was far older than that, built on as hundreds of years of mothers passing down practical advice to their daughters.

Many medical historians think that midwives were far safer and more successful at delivering healthy children because they were generally more sanitary than doctors. Before society understood the concept of germs, midwives had careful habits of washing and cleaning themselves. Unfortunately, as the century went on, male doctors pushed midwives aside and took control of the medical market. Often they used what seemed like more advanced technology—forceps for delivering babies, fancy medicines—to win patients away from midwifes.

EYEWITNESS ACCOUNT

The following is from a speech by Sojourner Truth, a free black woman who spent her life advocating equal rights for women and blacks and others. The speech, titled "Ain't I A Woman?" was given at a women's convention in Akron, Ohio, 1851:

Well, children, where there is so much racket there must be something out of kilter. I think that 'twixt the negroes of the South and the women at the North, all talking about rights, the white men will be in a fix pretty soon. But what's all this here talking about?

That man over there says that women need to be helped into carriages, and lifted over ditches, and to have the best place everywhere. Nobody ever helps me into carriages, or over mud-puddles, or gives me any best place! And ain't I a woman? Look at me! Look at my arm! I have ploughed and planted, and gathered into barns, and no man could head me! And ain't I a woman? I could work as much and eat as much as a man—when I could get it—and bear the lash as well! And ain't I a woman? I have borne thirteen children, and seen most all sold off to slavery, and when I cried out with my mother's grief, none but Jesus heard me! And ain't I a woman?

Skilled Trades

Many of the jobs done today by machines or in factories were once done by skilled workers. Usually, these workers did their jobs in towns or cities. Often, these trades required an apprenticeship—meaning a young person would spend time learning the skill from an older person who had been doing the job a long time. In this way, skills were passed down from generation to generation. Fathers and mothers also taught sons and daughters their trades, ensuring the family business continued.

Leatherworkers

Leatherworkers had made their living in America since its earliest days, when animal hides were brought into the towns from French and Native trappers. The 1800s saw the great slaughter of the bison on the Plains, as well as a continued demand for leather clothing and equipment. Tanners transformed the ancient practice of curing a hide into a skilled profession.

Animal hides had to first be stretched, then soaked in various oozes and syrup concoctions. A common ingredient in the mix was tannic acid from tree bark, which is where the tanner got his name. Once the hides had soaked, they were scraped clean of excess fur and then soaked again to destroy bacteria. The raw, tanned hide was then dried out and passed on to other skilled tradesmen who would use it for various purposes.

Specialist leatherworkers were known as curriers. They took tanned

Leatherworkers used sharp tools to scrape all the fur and flesh from hides.

leather and applied colored dyes, then stretched or reworked it to make the leather softer and more attractive. Often these more refined leathers went to other trades such as saddle makers, bridle makers, shoemakers, or glovemakers.

Potters

Pottery and ceramics were another skilled trade of the 1800s, and potters and stoneworkers were in every major city of the 1800s. There was a huge demand for stoneware of all shapes and sizes.

Stoneware, which was often made from clay mixtures, was used to make containers for water, beer, meat, grain, jelly, pickled vegetables, as well as items like pitchers, butter pots, and water coolers—all the jars and containers that today would be made from plastic or glass. Specialized stoneworkers made beautiful pots with elaborate designs, or more unusual items like birdhouses and animal figurines.

Shoemakers sewed shoes out of pieces of leather.

Potters and stoneworkers created the many types of containers used in everyday life.

Tailors and Seamstresses

In the 1800s, tailors and seamstresses made and mended clothing. Most cloth in the early nineteenth century was woven not in America but in Europe. Cloth was one of American's largest imports, and was used by tailors and seamstresses to create clothes for both the rich and poor.

The rich demanded that European styles of dress be imitated in America, and tailors were paid large sums to cut and sew cloth into precise shapes and sizes. It was common in those days for a tailor to design an entire outfit for a particular person. The concept of mass-produced clothing was still in the future. Instead, people sought out tailors famous for their handiwork.

Dentists

Dentistry was another trade of the day, one that was still being refined and formalized. America had some of the earliest schools of dentistry; one opened in Baltimore, Maryland, in 1840, and another in Philadelphia in 1863.

For centuries, dentists had been feared—and in some cases, despised—for the pain they inflicted on their patients. The most common solution for an aching tooth was to simply pull it out. This usually solved the problem, but in

Well-to-do men and women in the 1800s depended on their tailors and seamstresses to keep them dressed at the height of fashion.

If you had gone to a dentist in the 1800s, his office might have looked much like this.

the process, the patient experienced a great deal of pain and sometimes damage to the area around the tooth.

Dentists were sometimes known as "barber-surgeons" who would go from town to town offering their services to anyone who had a minor injury, wanted an aching tooth removed—or needed a haircut! As the 1800s advanced, patient treatment improved as dentists got better tools and better education. More dentists were able to make a living by concentrating only on dentistry, and in cities and larger towns, they set up offices. Still, their profession remained mostly limited to pulling teeth.

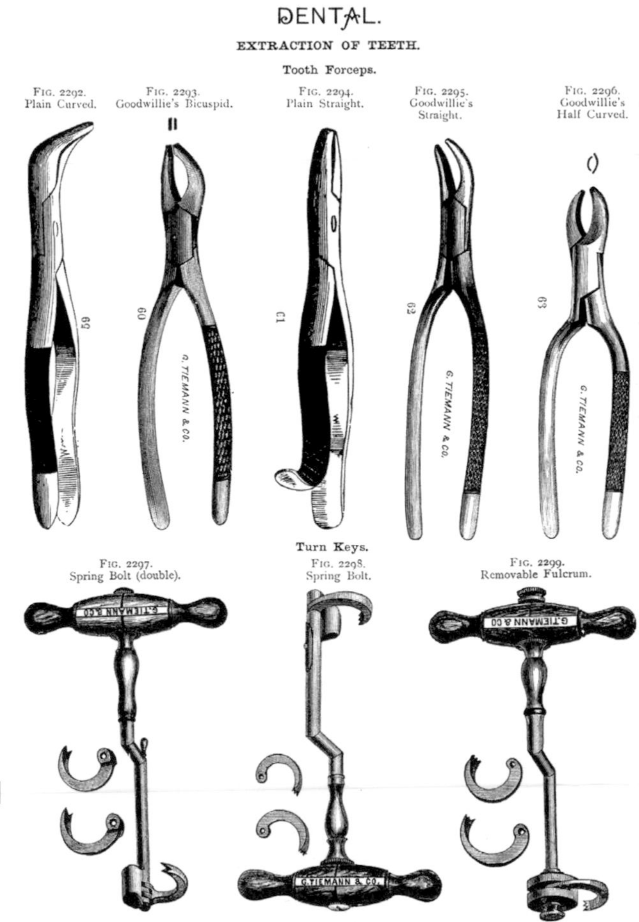

The best dentists of the 1800s usually had a set of tools like this one, designed for pulling teeth as efficiently as possible.

African Americans at Work

Forced slave labor can hardly be called an occupation, and yet the U.S. economy depended for many years on the hard work of African slaves. Blacks on plantations and small slave-holding farms worked in the fields and in the slave owner's households. They did almost all the work of the farm, planting, maintaining, and harvesting the crops. After the Civil War, many of the freed slaves went on to start farms of their own, having known no other occupation for most of their lives.

A growing group of free blacks lived in the North in the years before the Civil War. Blacks fought in the Revolutionary War and the War of 1812, and some owned land, homes, businesses, and paid taxes. A few blacks even owned their own plantations and their own slaves.

Free blacks were often outspoken on the issues of freedom and slavery. Many were key "conductors" on the Underground Railroad, using their homes and resources to hide escaped slaves. Other blacks attacked slavery in print, publishing newspapers such as *Freedom's Journal*, a paper started in 1827 to work against slavery by defending the intellectual ability of African Americans.

Much of America's wealth was built on the labor of blacks who were brought to this country against their will.

EYEWITNESS ACCOUNT

The Diary of a Slave

Josiah Henson spent thirty years on a plantation in Montgomery County, Maryland before he escaped slavery and became a Methodist preacher, abolitionist, lecturer, and founder of a cooperative colony of former slaves in Canada. His memoirs were published in 1849.

My earliest employments were, to carry buckets of water to the men at work, and to hold a horse-plough, used for weeding between the rows of corn. As I grew older and taller, I was entrusted with the care of master's saddle-horse. Then a hoe was put into my hands, and I was soon required to do the day's work of a man; and it was not long before I could do it, at least as well as my associates in misery.

The principal food of those upon my master's plantation consisted of corn-meal and salt herrings; to which was added in summer a little buttermilk, and the few vegetables which each might raise for himself and his family, on the little piece of ground which was assigned to him for the purpose, called a truck-patch.

In ordinary times we had two regular meals in a day: breakfast at twelve o'clock, after laboring from daylight, and supper when the work of the remainder of the day was over. In harvest season we had three. Our dress was of tow-cloth; for the children, nothing but a shirt; for the older ones a pair of pantaloons or a gown in addition, according to the sex. Besides these, in the winter a round jacket or overcoat, a wool-hat once in two or three years, for the males, and a pair of coarse shoes once a year.

We lodged in log huts, and on the bare ground. Wooden floors were an unknown luxury. In a single room were huddled, like cattle, ten or a dozen persons, men, women, and children. All ideas of refinement and decency were, of course, out of the question. We had neither bedsteads, nor furniture of any description. Our beds were collections of straw and old rags, thrown down in the corners and boxed in with boards; a single blanket the only covering. Our favourite way of sleeping, however, was on a plank, our heads raised on an old jacket and our feet toasting before the smouldering fire. The wind whistled and the rain and snow blew in through the cracks, and the damp earth soaked in the moisture till the floor was miry as a pig-sty. Such were our houses. In these wretched hovels were we penned at night, and fed by day; here were the children born and the sick neglected.

EXTRA! EXTRA!

Attention citizens of Pittsburgh, Pennsylvania: the new canal, under construction since 1826, is now completed! City officials tell us that our growing iron and glass industries will profit enormously from the new canal and its connection to Philadelphia and to the other great cities of the East.

The canal will connect to the Allegheny and Monongahela rivers, which already meet in Pittsburgh where they create the mighty Ohio River that leads to the West. As every citizen of Pittsburgh knows, the massive coal deposits at Coal Hill near the city make us an invaluable player in the industry of this nation. The first steamboat, The New Orleans, was built in Pittsburgh, connecting us to the rich port of New Orleans in the south, and now we are connected to the east as well. Already men are pouring into the city to fill the many positions needed in glass and ironmaking, textiles, furniture making, and distilling.

With the arrival of the canal, citizens of Pittsburgh can rest assured that shipbuilding will continue to be the pride of our young city. Already men are being contracted to build ships for New York and for the new Erie Canal. The new canal secures a spot for Pittsburgh as one of the nation's fastest growing cities.

Part II
Frontiersmen, Miners, Cowboys, & Soldiers

By the middle of the 1800s, white settlers were exploring more and more of the North American continent. Their maps were filling in with places, names, and details about the land. The Western region had its advocates, many of whom were economically invested in the area. These were restaurant owners and food distributors, ship owners and railroad tycoons. Anyone who stood to make money from the population of the West was likely to sing its praises, luring settlers from the East.

Land advertisements like this were designed to lure settlers to the frontier.

That's why pioneers going West by land needed guides, men who had made many trips before, who knew the many trails well, and who knew the advantages and disadvantages of each trail. The settlers needed guides to help them plan their provisions—what foods to pack, how much to pack, what kind

Towns sprang up all along the trail west, and storekeepers made their living supplying settlers with the things they needed for their journeys.

The city of Denver, Colorado, was built in the 1800s to supply settlers with the goods and services they needed.

EYEWITNESS ACCOUNT

From the diary of Demas Barnes
Denver, Colorado, June 27, 1865

Denver is a square, proud, prompt little place, which, like Pompey's Pillar, is surrounded by immensity. It is better built than St. Joseph or Atchison, has fine brick stores, four churches, a good seminary, two theatres, two banks, plenty of gambling shops, a fine United States mint, which I observed had nothing to do, and which, as near as I could ascertain, had actually coined the vast amount of forty thousand dollars in a whole year! and the most abominable hotels a person ever put his feet into. There being no wood, brick becomes a necessity for building purposes—hence the character of its buildings. Population claimed, six thousand. I am sorry to cut them down to four thousand, but that is more than they can count, unless they add the flies, of which at least several millions dine with us every day.

of animals and supplies to bring—as well as prepare against attacks by Native Americans, sickness, storms, and other emergencies. In fact, a whole business grew up around the pioneers' needs. Small towns sprang up in places nearby the long trails West where the shopkeepers and store owners made most of their money from travelers stopping to re-supply and rest.

Gold!

The discovery of gold in the West led to entire towns being built to meet the needs of gold miners. Gold miners were known as "prospectors" because so often they came looking for the prospect (or possibility) of gold. Rumors circulated, telling of vast riches of gold in California, and of men striking it rich in one swoop of a pickaxe. Some of the stories were true, but most were not.

The men they attracted were usually single men, able to travel cheaply and quickly in hopes of becoming wealthy overnight. Most remained poor, but in the meantime their presence in Western towns meant new jobs were needed. Without them, when winter came, the miners would be left to face snow and freezing temperatures.

Restaurants were in high demand, as were hotels. For the most part, these single men did not cook or keep house, so many "hospitality" jobs were born in the West. Men and women prepared meals that were both expensive and lavish (for the occasional man who had struck it rich) as well as simple and plain for the ordinary miner. People made their livings renting rooms, keeping house, and ordering supplies of food, medicine, and clothing. Long after the gold rush died down, many of the hotels and restaurants lived on, and remain to this day some of the oldest establishments in the West.

Restaurants, hotels, and grocery stores catered to miners' needs. Men without any women with them were especially apt to eat their meals in restaurants.

EXTRA! EXTRA!

Prospectors, Take Notice: Are You Ready for the Winter?

Frank Leslie's Illustrated Newspaper
August 20, 1859

In a short time, probably by the middle of October, this whole region will be snowed under and frozen up, so as to put a stop to the working of sluices if not mining altogether. There, then, for a period of at least six months, will be no employment . . . and for those who are without provisions or money, there is literally nothing left but starvation.

Cowboys and Cow Towns

Meanwhile, in Texas and New Mexico, people were making a living by answering the demand for beef. In San Francisco in the West, and in the major cities of the East, people wanted more meat.

Texans moved huge herds of cattle to slaughterhouses in Chicago to be shipped around the world. For the first time, huge profits could be made by driving cattle long distances. The trick was getting the herd there without losing too many to sickness or attack; this was the cowboy's job. Ranchers raised, captured, or bought their cattle, and when they had a herd big enough for a drive, they entrusted it to a few cowboys. The cowboys guided the herd through storms and into pastures to feed. They camped with the herd and

Texas cattle were driven into Dodge City, Kansas, where they could be shipped by train to other parts of the country. Dodge became the cattle capital of the West—and it was the wildest and roughest of all the cattle towns.

Cowboys were known for letting off steam when they came into town. Because their high spirits could turn violent, many cow towns required that cowboys coming in from a cattle drive check their guns with the sheriff.

carried weapons against predators and other attacks.

Similar to the gold-rush towns in the West, "cow towns" sprang up in the middle states to support the cattle industry. Usually they were located at important "railheads" where cowboys could load their herds onto trains headed for Chicago. Cow towns supported barbers and barkeeps, cooks and tailors. A cowboy who'd just finished his long journey and been paid could spend his new earnings right then and there on a haircut, a drink, a fine meal, or new pair of pants.

EYEWITNESS ACCOUNT

The following is from the diary of a Sergeant in the Thirty-Fifth Regiment of the Massachusetts Volunteers during the Civil War. His name was Henry, and in this entry he describes an ordinary day for a soldier from the North.

September 10th.

Have been on the move off and on since the 7th. Are now encamped near Brookville, MD waiting for rations. Weather has been very warm causing many to fall out on the march. We have no tents yet, but get on quite comfortable with blankets. A rain, however, would not be quite so comfortable to us. Before leaving our camp spot of the 7th, our Colonel told us in an address to the regiment that there was some prospect of getting into action soon. Exhorted us to be cool, to have our ears open for orders and our eyes about us, and not be watching where this or that shell or solid shot was going to strike. Said he was perfectly willing we should forage our food whenever we were short for rations whether in the enemies' country or not, but to be sure and not waste anything, foraging enough for our immediate wants and no more. Are restricted today to what we can pick up for our food, as supply trains are not up with us. Have lived on fried apples and potatoes mostly today. Wrote letter to folks at home. Feel I ought to have written more of the near prospect of our getting into a fight, of my feelings and some parting words to them. Think it would be well to write something of these and seal up and in case of my death in action have them sent to them.

Part III
Factory Workers and Industry

Things changed significantly for men and women when an economic depression hit the country in the 1820s. With farm economies suffering, jobs in the new factories began to look more appealing.

Lowell Mills in Massachusetts was one of the first factories in America to employ many women. By 1840, the factory employed almost 8,000 workers, mostly women between the ages of sixteen and thirty-five. Work in the textile mills in the early 1800s was hard. Workers spent long hours on their feet surrounded by noisy machines. Yet, the mills were generally clean and orderly.

By the second half of the 1800s, more and more American women were working in factories.

From B. H. Penhallow's Printing Establishment,

Wyman's Exchange, Cor. Merrimack & Central Sts.

TIME TABLE

1868.

OF THE LOWELL MILLS,

Arranged to make the working time 66 hours per week. The STANDARD TIME will be marked at noon, by the BELL of the MERRIMACK MANUFACTURING COMPANY.

Breakfast,..........at.......... 6. A. M.
Commence Work,.........."........... 6.30 A. M.
Dinner,............................12 M.
Commence Work, after Dinner, at..........12.45 P. M.
Stop Work, except on Saturday Evenings, at.... 6.30 P. M.

BELLS.

Morning Bells.	Dinner Bells.
First Bell,..........4.30 A. M.	Ring Out,..........12.00 M.
Second Bell,..........5.30 A. M.	Ring in,..........12.35 P. M.
Third Bell,..........6.20 A. M.	

Evening Bells.

Ring Out,.....6.30 P. M.......Except on Saturday Evenings.

SATURDAY EVENING BELL, 5 P. M.

YARD GATES will be opened at the first stroke of the bells for entering or leaving the Mills.

Speed Gates commence hoisting three minutes before commencing work.

For factory workers, Lowell Mills was considered to be one of the fairest and healthiest. This actual schedule from the factory shows that the women who were employed there still worked long hard hours.

The company hired young women from farms near the mills. The Lowell girls, as they came to be called, usually sent their wages home to their families. At first, parents hesitated to let their daughters work in the mills, so the company built boardinghouses to make parents feel better about sending their daughters to work. The company also made rules to protect the young women. Companies like Lowell Mills set high standards for quality working conditions. Unfortunately, Lowell would prove to be unusual in the late 1800s, when a growing number of factory owners treated their workers poorly.

The depression of the 1820s attracted men to the industrial sector too. For the first time, women and men were entering the same workplace—the "industrial" workplace—at about the same rate. Hard times were the great equalizer. In addition to factory jobs, women often left home to take support positions like secretaries or nannies, anything to bring more money to the household.

These women worked in a textile mill. The work was hard and exhausting (and sometimes dangerous).

The Changing Face of America

The Industrial Revolution was in full swing by the end of the 1800s in America. Calling it a "revolution" makes it sound like it happened overnight, but that isn't quite true. Throughout the 1800s, more machines were being introduced into the workplace. Railroads were expanding like a web to the far corners of the United States. Slowly but surely, America changed from a rural to an urban society. More people moved to the cities looking for jobs, usually leaving a farming life behind.

They weren't alone, either. Huge immigrant populations from Ireland, Poland, Germany, and Italy arrived in the new cities in waves. They too were looking for city jobs.

The U.S. population was swelling, creating a demand for more products, and the population of cities was growing at the same pace. From the year 1800 to the year 1890, the U.S. population grew from about 5 million people to 63 million people, more than twelve times its original size! And most of

During the 1800s, cities like Minneapolis, Minnesota, grew, as more and more Americans became urban workers.

Immigrants often lived in tenements like those shown here. The housing was crowded, and fire was a constant danger.

these new citizens lived in cities, where they worked at jobs that were far removed from the farming work so common at the end of the eighteenth century.

The "revolution" was not kind to everyone. New conditions in cities meant new opportunities, but not all of them were good. As industry boomed and new jobs arrived, so did the workplace dangers and negligence of bad employers. Unions formed to protect people from abuse, and reformers entered the cities, arguing for better living conditions for the extremely poor immigrants. While the Industrial Revolution may have allowed the United States to grow into a powerful nation, it did so at the expense of its poorest classes of people.

Kids at Work

Child labor played a huge role in the Industrial Revolution. At the end of the nineteenth century, the U.S. Census found that about 2 million American children worked in mills, farms, factories, and on the city streets.

Children were put to work in all kinds of places. In mills, they started working as young as five years old. Their small size made them perfect for dangerous tasks like climbing atop a spinning frame to mend broken threads or put back empty bobbins. They worked from 7 a.m. to 5:30 p.m. and sometimes much longer, usually for less than 50 cents a day. The children who worked in the mines started working when they were five years old, pulling cartloads of coal through tight passages. Their lives were so unhealthy and dangerous that most

These boys worked in a factory during the late 1800s, doing odd jobs like sweeping the floors.

weren't expected to live past twenty-five.

Children did odd jobs of all kinds: they carried boxes of hats for a retail store, or in coastal cities they shucked oysters and picked shrimp for a few dollars a month. Some children were bootblacks in the cities, carrying a rag and a tin of polish, stopping wealthy men to shine their shoes. Others were "bowling alley boys" who worked well past midnight, setting up pins for the bowlers. Sometimes they were orphans, brought from far away to work in cities for a boss who'd adopted them into a kind of forced labor. Sometimes they simply needed to make a few extra cents for their poor families.

One famous example of child labor in the late 1800s was the arrival of "newsies" in many cities. These were usually young boys who'd been employed to sell newspapers. When they weren't looking for food or selling papers, these young boys often gambled and drank alcohol in the streets with older men. Older boys and men frequently encouraged the youngest boys to steal, smoke, and drink.

Some newsboys started at a very young age. This boy looks to be about five or six.

Snapshot from the Past

The Life of a Factory Child

Jimmy Barns was born in the year 1875—and five years later, he went to work in a metal factory. By the time he was twelve, he was as exhausted as an old man. He never had time to play; he seldom had enough to eat. But he had nine younger brothers and sisters, and his family depended on his income, small as it was.

On a hot summer day, Jimmy struggled to stay awake while doing the monotonous work that was his job. He had gotten up at four-thirty, begun

Young nineteenth-century factory workers lived exhausting lives.

work at five-thirty, and now, his head nodded—but he jerked awake when the overseer gave him a sharp rap on the head.

"You were nearly ten minutes late this morning," the overseer growled, "and now you're falling asleep on the job. I'm going to have to dock you a week's pay. We'll see if that teaches you to do the job you're being paid to do."

Tears sprang into Jimmy's eyes, but he blinked them away and went back to work.

At ten o'clock, the workers took a fifteen-minute break to eat their breakfast. Jimmy slurped down the thin soup and wolfed the dry piece of bread. Then he went back to work. He was dreading going home tonight and telling his mother that his pay would be docked. She would cry, he knew, because they were counting on his paycheck to buy groceries—and now the little ones would go hungry.

But by six o'clock that evening, Jimmy was too tired to think about anything except getting home. He trudged back to the crowded tenement where he lived with his family, eager to eat some supper and fall into bed.

Tomorrow, he would do it all again.

Coal Power

Beginning in the middle of the 1800s, when trains adapted to coal power and coal became a kind of "black gold," coal mining became a way of life for many Americans. In the late 1800s, coal was a very big business. Often entire towns were built around a single coal-mining company. Pennsylvania, Kentucky, West Virginia, Arkansas, and many more states all welcomed coal, thinking it would bring jobs and money to their economies.

Unfortunately, the workers paid the price. Mining was a dangerous job. Even today, stories of cave-ins and explosions are not uncommon. Workdays were very long in the mines, twelve hours or more, with Saturday being a shorter day and Sunday being the only day off.

Mining was dangerous on many levels. First, there was the constant coal dust that caused frequent respiratory illnesses. This was the cause of what was known as the "miner's cough." If the cough didn't kill the miners early in life, they usually developed a mine-related illness later in life, such as lung

Miners lived most of their lives underground, working in a dangerous and unhealthy environment.

This photograph shows nineteenth-century coal miners installing beams to hold up the ceiling.

EYEWITNESS ACCOUNT

A Miner's Wife

Oh yes, the men would go for weeks without seeing daylight sometimes. We wives would take the lunch buckets to the mine and hand them to the lamp man, and he would give us the old bucket, and they'd give the men the food. Oh yes, many a day we did that, three times a day. Weeks went by when I only knew I had a husband because those food buckets came back to me empty.

(Adapted from an oral history from Explore Pennsylvania History.)

cancer or a respiratory disease called silicosis. In addition, they constantly faced the danger of collapsing tunnels and wooden structures. Often, the only thing between a miner and tons of rock and earth was a wooden fence.

A gas referred to as "firedamp" lurked in mines, a highly explosive gas that could be ignited by the slightest spark or friction. Mine owners had to hire special workers, called "blowers," to get rid of this gas. Their job was to monitor pits for firedamp and for another dangerous gas called "afterdamp," which we know today as carbon monoxide. Carbon monoxide is poisonous and if it accumulates, it can kill a person. These gases were removed by furnaces and steam, burning them off in small batches, or by ventilating the shafts so that the gases were allowed to escape. Even so, the gases could be deadly to the men who worked below ground.

Miners often did not live long. And yet mining was a way of life that swallowed up the males of entire families who were struggling to make enough money to support themselves.

EXTRA! EXTRA!

Mine Strike!
The New York Times
Little Rock, Ark., May 4, 1899

Gov. Jones has been informed of a movement to bring into the coal mining district an armed body of men to take the places of the strikers.

The Governor has given instructions to State authorities to summon every able-bodied man in Sebastian County, if necessary, to enforce the injunction of Judge Rowe prohibiting the importation of laborers.

All such armed men are to be met at the State line and placed under arrest, as are also those who supply the arms. Mine operators will also be arrested by State authorities when they attempt to bring in armed laborers under protection of Deputy Marshals.

The injunctions issued by the State and Federal courts are in direct conflict and the Governor regards the situation as critical. He is determined that the writ of the State court shall be carried, and if necessary will go to the mining district in person and direct the carrying out of the court's order, which he believes to be the only way in which bloodshed can be avoided. The strikers are armed, and sanguinary conflict is believed to be inevitable if non-union men are imported.

Coal miners rode on small trains like this down into the earth where they did their jobs.

New Technologies

Many of the things we take for granted today—rapid transportation, telecommunications, and crowded cities built high into the sky—are actually inventions of the 1800s. Each of them brought new occupations to America's workforce.

Take the telephone, for instance. By the end of the 1800s, telegraph and telephone wires were strung across every major city in America. With the arrival of new technology came the need for people who knew how to use it. For a while telegraph specialists were hired in places like New York City, usually men who sent messages in Morse code (named for Samuel Morse, who invented the telegraph) between offices and factories. Eventually, however, the telephone replaced the telegraph, and therefore interpreters who knew Morse code were no longer needed. The telephone allowed people to communicate in their own voices to other people hundreds of miles away. Being a telephone operator was a new job that was open to women.

The first telephone operators were teenage boys, who often engaged in horseplay and foul language. Telephone companies soon began hiring young women instead, in order to present a more genteel image to customers.

INCREDIBLE INDIVIDUAL
Alexander Graham Bell

We remember Alexander Graham Bell as the inventor of the telephone, but he was actually a brilliant and curious scientist whose interests extended far beyond the invention that brought him fame and fortune.

Bell invented the telephone when he was only twenty-nine years old. A year later, in 1877, he formed the Bell Telephone Company. His future was secure, and he was able to arrange his life so he could devote himself to his scientific interests. He was driven by curiosity, and throughout his entire life, he continued to search, learn, and create.

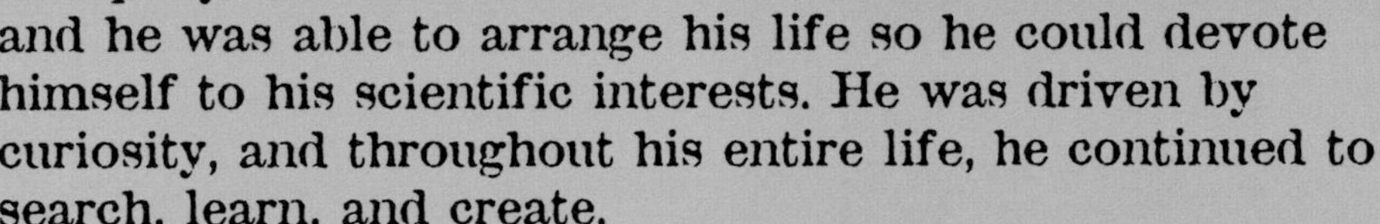

One of his innovations was the "photophone," a device that enabled sound to be transmitted on a beam of light. Bell and his assistant developed the photophone using a sensitive selenium crystal and a mirror that would vibrate in response to a sound. In 1881, they successfully sent a photophone message over 200 yards from one building to another. Bell regarded the photophone as "the greatest invention I have ever made; greater than the telephone." Today's laser and fiber optic communication systems are built on the principles Bell discovered.

Over the years, Alexander Graham Bell's curiosity would lead him to speculate on many far-ranging scientific questions, from heredity to artificial respiration. His most long-lasting interest, however, was the challenge of flight. Months before he died, Bell told a reporter, "There cannot be mental atrophy in any person who continues to observe, to remember what he observes, and to seek answers for his unceasing hows and whys about things."

Steel

In our world today, we take steel for granted, forgetting that it is a relatively recent invention, born in American during the late 1800s. The demand came from the railroads, which needed steel to make their rails. By the end of the nineteenth century, largely through the efforts of Andrew Carnegie, the United States made more steel than anyone else in the world and sold it at the lowest cost. Carnegie made his fortune not by creating a new technique for forging

Because of the fires required to melt the metal, steel mills were extremely hot.

Steelworkers had exhausting and often dangerous jobs.

steel, but by producing it on a massive scale, the likes of which had never been seen before.

The life of a steelworker was hard. Steelworkers endured twelve-hour shifts, seven days a week. Andrew Carnegie gave his workers only one holiday in the year—the Fourth of July. Many workers went without breaks, only stopping to oil the engine. During oiling, some took a break for a fast lunch, but others simply didn't have time. Because steelwork was so grueling, there were few old men in a steel factory. "Old age at forty," is what they called it. Working near furnaces all day made for extremely hot conditions. One worker remarked of the heat: "It sweats the life out of a man. I often drink two buckets of water during twelve hours; the sweat drips through my sleeves, and runs down my legs and fills my shoes."

For all their hard work, steelworkers usually earned a measly $10 a week, just above the poverty line of $500 a year. It would have taken the paychecks of 4,000 men to match the yearly earnings of their boss, Andrew Carnegie.

Snapshot from the Past

Another Perspective

Rose's real name was Jariuk Uklenk—but only her family still called her that. At school, the teachers called her Rose, and she used that name when she began working in the hospital laundry during her summer vacations.

Rose had spent most of her life in Carlisle Boarding School in Pennsylvania. There she had been taught to forget the Cherokee ways practiced by her family at home. The teachers taught the students how to read and write and do arithmetic, and then they helped the students get jobs. They also taught the students to worship the white men's God.

Rose knew she should feel grateful to the school—but instead, she often felt angry. She had heard the school's founder, Richard Henry Pratt, give a speech where he said, "A great general has said that the only good Indian is a dead one. In a sense, I agree with the sentiment, but only in this: that all the Indian there is in the race should be dead. Kill the Indian in him and save the man." Sometimes Rose wished that the Indian in her had not been killed. She missed her family, but when she went home, she no longer knew how to understand them—and they could no longer understand her.

"We are walking ghosts," her grandfather had told her the last time she had been allowed to go home for a visit. "Our wars are over. The white man has won. He has spread across this entire land, and we can no longer fight. We are as good as dead." Tears had rolled down his wrinkled face, and Rose had felt that same mixed-up feeling she had so often: a combination of guilt and anger and sorrow.

When Rose graduated from the Carlisle school, she knew the teachers would make sure she had a job in one of the nearby towns. She would work in a laundry like the one where she worked now or some other place, and she would earn money to send to her family on the reservation where they lived. She was glad she could do at least that much for them.

As America grew in size and population, Native Americans were pushed off their lands again and again. The last of the Indian Wars had been fought (and lost by the Native tribes) by the end of the 1800s, and Indian boarding schools like the one at Carlisle, Pennsylvania, were an attempt to reconcile Native people to their new lot in life. The boarding schools taught trades to their students, so that when they graduated they could help fill the demand for labor in America's growing cities.

An Era of Change

We think of our modern world as an era of great change and innovation, but the 1800s witnessed changes that were just as impressive and life shaking. The development of railroads, for example, brought some of the nineteenth century's most dramatic changes. In only twenty-five years, almost 70,000 miles of tracks were laid—and this meant that new jobs and lifestyles were created across America. More goods could now be produced in factories because the market for those goods had expanded, since the railroads could carry them across the country. Railroads even changed the way Americans ate; for the first time, fresh produce was available all over the nation year-round. Farms expanded in size to meet the growing markets in the cities.

The invention of electricity transformed the work world as well by extending the workday. Factories could now be open after dark. Productivity soared, and the nation grew rich. While more and more white Americans moved to the West, settling the continent, the immigrants who flocked to America's cities met the growing demand for a larger work force.

The success of today's America is rooted in the 1800s. Unfortunately, many of our modern problems, such as urban crime, poverty, and racial injustice, are rooted there as well. By the end of the 1800s, the nation was poised to enter the twentieth century, where it would take on new and more powerful roles on the global stage—and face new challenges. America was filled with a spirit of optimism, a willingness to tackle even the biggest problems, and that too has carried over into our world today.

Think About It

There are many differences between the working world of the 1800s and the twenty-first century. In the nineteenth century, the average American worker worked much longer hours, often in dangerous conditions, had far fewer "benefits" (health insurance, vacation days, unemployment insurance), and had little chance for advancement. Women, African Americans, and new immigrants were stuck at the bottom of the "job ladder," and even middle-class white men had far fewer career choices.

- Since schooling beyond elementary school was unusual, what do you think the average person of about your age was doing in the 1800s?
- How do you think going to work at an early age affected childhood and adolescence for most Americans?
- How do you think work would have affected the way these young workers felt about themselves, their lives, and their futures?
- Can you think of any ways a talented young person in the 1800s could better themselves and find opportunities for success?

Words Used in This Book

advocates: People or groups who argue for and support an idea or cause.

atrophy: Decline or deterioration; wasting away.

commerce: Business, trade, an exchange of goods.

depression (economic): A period of time during which there is higher unemployment and less business being conducted.

domestic: Relating to the home or household.

economies: The earnings and resources of particular places or industries.

formalized: Given a specific shape or form; defined; often in regards to an activity or idea.

gender: Relating to categories of male and female.

imports: Things that are brought in from other countries to use and sell.

injunction: A legal order commanding a person or group to do or not do something.

innovations: Things, or ways of doing things, that are new and different.

mass-produced: Goods that are made in large numbers, especially using machines.

memoirs: An autobiography; a collection of stories from a person's life.

merchants: People who buy and sell goods to make a living.

negligence: Not taking care of something or someone a person is responsible for.

optimism: A tendency to look at the good instead of the bad and a belief that a good outcome will occur.

productivity: A measure of how much is accomplished compared to how much effort has been put into a job.

refined: Made more pure or precise.

reformers: People who work to make something better.

reservation: A piece of land set aside by the United States government for use by a Native American tribe.

sanguinary: Bloody.

sector: A part or section of something larger.

seminary: A school to train people to become religious leaders; also, a secondary school for young women.

sentiment: Attitude, opinion, or emotion.

textile: A material that can be woven into cloth, or else the cloth woven from such a material.

transformed: Changed dramatically, in form appearance, or characteristic.

tycoons: A wealthy and powerful businessperson.

urban: Relating to a city or town.

writ: An order issued by an official that requires a specific action.

Find Out More

In Books

Bartoletti, Susan Campbell. *Kids on Strike!* New York: Sandpiper, 2003.

Burgan, Michael. *American Newsboy.* Mankato, Minn.: Compass Point, 2007.

Flanagan, Alice K. *The Lowell Mill Girls.* Mankato, Minn.: Compass Point, 2005.

Kalman, Bobby and Kate Calder. *The Life of a Miner.* New York: Crabtree Publishing, 2000.

Oatman, Eric. *Cowboys on the Western Trail: The Cattle Drive Adventures of Joshua McNabb and Davy Bartlett.* Washington, D.C.: National Geographic Children's Books, 2004.

Ratliff, Tom. *You Wouldn't Want to Work on the Brooklyn Bridge! An Enormous Project that Seemed Impossible.* New York: Franklin Watts, 2010.

Thornton, Jeremy. *New Industries, New Jobs: British Immigrants Come to America, 1830s–1890s.* New York: PowerKids Press, 2004.

On the Internet

19th Century Doctors in the U.S.
rosemelnickmuseum.wordpress.com/2009/03/11/19th-century-doctors-in-the-us

Childhood Lost: Child Labor During the Industrial Revolution
www.eiu.edu/~eiutps/childhood.php

A Cowboy in Dodge City, 1882
www.eyewitnesstohistory.com/dodge.htm

From Cellar to Shingles: Early 19th-Century Building Trades
www.connerprairie.org/Learn-And-Do/Indiana-History/America-1800-1860/19th-Century-Building-Trades.aspx

Life in the Mines: The Life of an Immigrant Miner
www.iarelative.com/mines.htm

The Mill Girls: Lowell Mills During the Industrial Revolution
www.berwickacademy.org/millgirls/mill_girls.htm

Rise of Industrial America: Work in the Late 19th Century
memory.loc.gov/learn//features/timeline/riseind/work/work.html

The websites listed on this page were active at the time of publication. The publisher is not responsible for websites that have changed their address or discontinued operation since the date of publication. The publisher will review and update the websites upon each reprint.

Index

Picture Credits

Dover pp. 16–17, 18–19, 20–21, 22–23, 24–25, 26–27, 31, 32–33, 34–35, 36–37, 40–41
Explore Pennsylvania History pp. 54–55
Library and Archives Division, Historical Society of Western Pennsylvania pp. 54–55
Library of Congress pp. 22–23, 32–33, 38, 40–41, 42–43, 44–45
New York City Library Archives pp. 42–43
New York Public Library Archives pp. 28–29
New York State Archives p. 30
The Pennsylvania Anthracite Heritage Museum and Iron Furnaces pp. 48–49
Pennsylvania State Archives pp. 48–49, 50–51
Rose Melnick Medical Museum pp. 26–27
Telecommunications History pp. 52–53

To the best knowledge of the publisher, all images not specifically credited are in the public domain. If any image has been inadvertently uncredited, please notify Harding House Publishing Service, 220 Front Street, Vestal, New York 13850, so that credit can be given in future printings.

About the Author and the Consultant

Zachary Chastain is an independent writer and actor living in Binghamton, New York. He is the author of various educational books for both younger and older audiences.

John Gillis is a Rutgers University Professor of History Emeritus. A graduate of Amherst College and Stanford University, he has taught at Stanford, Princeton, University of California at Berkeley, as well as Rutgers. Gillis is well known for his work in social history, including pioneering studies of age relations, marriage, and family. The author or editor of ten books, he has also been a fellow at both St. Antony's College, Oxford, and Clare Hall, Cambridge.